JOURNAL OF LIEUTENANT ROBERT PARKER, OF THE SECOND CONTINENTAL ARTILLERY, 1779.

By Robert Parker

Reprinted by New York History Review
2019

Journal of Lieutenant Robert Parker, of The Second Continental Artillery, 1779

Excerpted from *Journals of the Military Expedition of Major General John Sullivan against the Six Nations of Indians in 1779* by Frederick Cook. Contributed by Thomas R. Bard.

Copyright ©2019 New York History Review. Some rights reserved.

Printed in the United States of America
First Edition

ISBN: 978-1-950822-04-1

To Newtown

Journal of Lieutenant Robert Parker

Journal of Lieutenant Robert Parker, of The Second Continental Artillery, 1779.

September 7th. — Marched at 9 o'clock, the land low & very rich, the woods open. Arrived at the outlet of the lake, about 3 o'clock, P. M. Here we waited until 5 giving time for Gen. Hand & Maxwell to arrive at the Town of Canadesaga, which they did by a circuitous march & by different Route, judging the enemy were still in possession of it — two pieces of cannon were kept in the rear lest an attack should be made on that quarter ; we then crossed the outlet which was about 40 yards wide & proceeded round to the N.Yr. Corner — our march was detained until dark when we were oblidged to drag our pieces over Logs, Morasses &c, and arrived at the town about 10 o'clock, where the rest of the army were encamped — Canaugoe is situated about two miles from the lake (& three from the outlet) on a rising piece of ground & contained about fifty houses. It appears to be a very old settlement, there are a great number of apple & peach trees here, which we cut down & destroyed — a great quantity of corn was also destroyed. This lake is called Seneca Lake, & is about 36 miles long & from 3 to 6 wide — Exceedingly beautiful & affords the most delightful prospect. The banks in many places are high, but without rocks, the land on each side rising gradually & exceeding fertile on all sides. At about 8 miles distance on the East side lies the Cayuga Lake, nearly parallel, of the same dimensions, tho' not quite so beautiful. The waters of the Seneca lake, falling into the Cayuga, about two miles, above the outlet afterwards makes part of the *Trois Reveres* or Three Rivers — The land between these lakes near the head is pretty high, but falls gradually towards the outlet into a flat & low Country all the way intersperced with purling streams and well calculated for every species of Agriculture & no doubt but it will one day become no inconsiderable part of the western empire — Dist. to-day 13 miles —

September 8th. — Lay by — a Detachment was sent about 6 miles up the Seneca Lake, where they destroyed a town of about twenty houses. Likewise a number of fruit trees & a great quantity of corn, in the evening another detachment was sent to assist in destroying the corn &c —

September 9th. — This morning all the sick & invalids were sent back to the garrison at Tioga — Marched at 12 o'clock, the road continued good and pretty clear for 3 miles — then we entered into a very thick and deep swamp that continued the remainder of the day. Encamped on an eminence, that was clear of timber & filled with high grass — Dist. 7 miles —

September 10th. — Marched at 9 o'clock, the swamp continued for 5 miles further, then we entered into an open country, that was free from timber & plenty of grass — next we came to the side of a lake that appeared to be 10 or 12 miles long & 1 1/2 wide but very shallow — we then proceeded along the east side of it, about a mile to the N end where we crossed the outlet that made a considerable brook — about from this outlet we entered the Town of Veruneudaga which contained about thirty Houses, very good and lately built — these we immediately burnt & then encamped about a mile from there near several cornfields, which we likewise destroyed — Dist. 12 miles.

September 11th. — Marched at 6 o'clock, the land low but very thick of young timber for 3 miles. Then we asscended some rising ground that was clear of timber in many places & full of grass — passed several deep hollows, next we descended a long hill, passed through a meadow & crossed a brook which we supposed came out of a lake at some distance on our left, the land continued pretty clear. Arrived at Kannanyayen about 4 o'clock. There was an old town that contained a number of houses. This place is situated on a large plain between two lakes — here was also a number of fruit trees & a large cornfield — Dist. 13 J miles.

September 12th. — Rain in the morning prevented our marching until 12 — we then drew 4 days provision & leaving one piece of artillery, all our Baggage, pack horses, drivers & Invalids proceeded. Crossed the outlet of a lake that appeared to be about 5 miles long & J broad; encamped at sunset in the woods, dist. 10 miles.

September 13th. — Marched at 6 o'clock, the morning very cold, in about 3 miles we arrived at a small Town, situated in a large plain called Egitsa, here was a great quantity of corn &c — At this place we halted until 10, in order to destroy the corn & build a bridge over a brook & morass about half a mile in front & otherwise impassable, previous to which Lieut. Boyd (of the Rifle corps) was detached with 25 men to a town about 6 miles further, where he arrived about daylight this morning — here he killed & scalped an Indian & wounded another — then returned towards camp, after having made all the discoveries he could. After they had travelled about 2 miles they agreed to lay by & wait the arrival of the army, but in the meantime sent two of the party to carry the Intelligence to the General. After the men had travelled about a mile, they saw Indians on the path before them, upon which they immediately retired back to their main body, they then all set out in order to return to the main army & if possible to come across the five Indians; after they had got within about a (?) of the army they saw another Indian, whom they killed & scalped likewise, but before done, they were all at once surrounded by a large body of Indians — Eleven of the party have returned, Lieut. Boyd with the remainder have not yet returned, & it is to be feared have fell a sacrifice to their barbarity — Upon hearing the firing the light Infantry were immediately ordered to reinforce ; after this the bridge being completed the army marched over the morass & asscended a very high hill. Just as our advance parties & Right flank were at the top of the hill, they discovered the Indians retreating, which they did with such precipitation as to leave the greatest part of their knapsacks & baggage behind, which fell into the hands of our men — On this hill we found the bodies of four of our men, that had been butchered by the enemy. McLodge, the Surveyor, & his party having advanced some distance in front of the army were fired at & one of the party shot through the body, who died the next morning. We then proceeded on through an exceeding high country to Cassawalaughlin about 6 miles ; on our arrival there we expected to meet the enemy. Accordingly we drew up in front of the town with our artillery where we halted some time, expecting to see the enemy with our right & left wings on the flanks & after some time advanced into the town, which we found evacuated ; fired three cannon, pitched our tents & lay till morning — dist. 9 miles.

September 14-th. — Got up at 3 o'clock & lay upon our arms until day in order to prevent a surprize. Large parties were detached to cut down the corn &c. Marched at 12 o'clock, crossed a large brook near the town, then entered into a most beautiful & extensive plain, which afforded an unbounded prospect ; here was almost a perfect level & nothing to obstruct the sight but a few spreading Oaks beautifully Intersperced & plenty of grass that grew spontaneous on every part & full six feet high. This plain is called the great Genesee plains & where we cross it was about 3 miles wide & runs to a great length. Near the west side runs the Seneca River about 80 yards wide & is a most beautiful plain. We then crossed it & proceeded by a N. course to the Genesee Town, which is about 3 miles down the river, & entered it about 5 o'clock; found it also evacuated. This town is situated near the river on a large fruitful plain & contained about eighty houses, some of which were very good. At this place we found the bodies of Lieut. Boyd and another, (mentioned yesterday) in a putrified & mangled condition. Lieut. Boyd was found with his head cut off & skinned all over, his eyes torn out, his nails pulled off, his body bruised & beat all over, & every other cruelty exercised upon him that malice & savage barbarity could invent, some of which are too shocking to relate. The greatest part of their cruelties appears to have been committed upon him while he was alive, in order to heighten his misery & satisfy their revenge. Thus died a good citizen, an agreeable friend & a gallant soldier — Inspired with every Heroe's virtue he fell a victim to their savage barbarity in defence of the injured rights of mankind. At dark he was inter'd with the Honors of war &c. — Dist. to-day, 5 miles.

September 15th. — At 6 o'clock the whole army was ordered to destroy the corn, which grew in amazing quantities in this place, with almost every kind of vegetables — which we entirely destroyed, first by collecting it & carrying it to the Houses, which we filled & then set on fire, & gathering large quantities of wood, mixed the corn with it in a pile & burnt it to ashes. At 12 we finished the destruction of the corn & likewise the business of the Expedition, when receiving the General's thanks, we set out on our return. At 3 we began our march almost in the same order reversed that we advanced in when repassing the river at same place we passed it the day before, entered on the plain and encamped on the Little Genesee.

September 16th. — Thus had we advanced 140 miles in the Enemy's country from Tioga and carried fire, sword and destruction in every part, that we could possibly find out or approach, in the prosecution of which, we had to encounter many and almost insurmountable difficulties, such as forcing a march all the way, cutting a Road for the Artillery, in many places a continued swamp for several miles, want of provisions, hard marches, and fatigue.

But here let us leave the busy army for a moment and suffer our imaginations to Run at large through these delightful wilds, & figure to ourselves the opening prospects of future greatness which we may reasonably suppose is not far distant, & that we may yet behold with a pleasing admiration those deserts that have so long been the habitation of beasts of prey & a safe asylum for our savage enemies, converted into fruitful fields, covered with all the richest productions of agriculture, amply rewarding the industrious husbandman by a golden harvest; the spacious plains abounding with flocks & herds to supply his necessary wants. These Lakes & Rivers that have for ages past rolled in sacred silence along their wonted course, unknown to Christian nations, produce spacious cities & guilded spires, rising on their banks, affording a safe retreat for the virtuous few that disdains to live in affluence at the expense of their liberties. The fish too, that have so long enjoyed a peaceful habitation in these transparent regions, may yet become subservient to the inhabitants of this delightful country.

Large detachments were sent out early this morning to destroy the remainder of the corn. Marched at 12 o'clock, Repassed the Little Genesee River, where we halted until the whole army crossed, then proceeding by the same route we had advanced, found the bodies of 14 of the party men- tioned the 13th inst. They were all found, tomahawked scalped & butchered in the most cruel manner; buried them, halted at Egitsa (mentioned the 13th), to destroy the remainder of the corn, encamped there &c.

September 17th. — Marched at 6 o'clock, passed the encampment & lake mentioned the 12th Inst., Arrived at Kenagaugus, where we found our baggage & provisions safe, which gave us great satisfaction, as we were under apprehensions that the enemy might take advantage of the weakness of the garrison & attempt to take possession of it, encamped there.

September 18th. — The General ordered us to be up at 5 but the great deficiency of Pack horses prevented our marching until 7, met by two Indians from Fort Schuyler, passed Keunandaga & encamped on the bank of the lake mentioned on the 11th inst.
vol. xxviii. — 2

September 19th. — Marched at 9, passed the encampment of the 9th & the swamp, encamped at Canasago about sunset — Dist. 16 miles. This day we were met by three men, who came express from Tioga, with dispatches for the General, they likewise gave acc'ts that there was plenty of provisions at that place, & that they had sent a quantity up the River as far as Newtown.

September 20th. — A detachment of 100 men & the command being ordered to force a march to Fort Schuyler, I agreed to go with them & accordingly we set out at 3 o'clock P.M., leaving the army encamped passed the end of the Seneca Lake to the outlet at the place we had crossed as Ave advanced, then proceeding down the river encamped at Scharoyos. This has been an Indian village & contained about twenty houses, which were burnt previous to our coming by a detachment of the army, it is situated on the bank of the Seneca outlet which at this place forms a beautiful River of about 50 yards wide. Here we got plenty of vegetables of almost every kind, potatoes in particular, & as we had now plenty of fresh beef & flour with us, we made an elegant repast, such as for a long time before we had been strangers to. About dark Coll. Butler arrived with a detachment of 600 men on an Expedition against the Cayuga settlements — dist. 9 miles.

September 21st. — Marched at sunrise, the country open & free from hills & withal very fertile for 6 miles — then we crossed some low land & deep swamps, arrived at the Cayuga Lake, 10 o'clock, dist. 10 miles. Crossed the mouth of the lake, which was about 400 yards wide & in most places 4 feet deep with, at least, a foot of mud in the bottom, then proceeding about a mile up the lake struck off near a N. E. corner. The country continued open for 10 miles & the timber chiefly oak, then we entered thick beech and Elm land, crossed the outlet of it & encamped on the bank. This lake is about a mile & a half in width and the length uncertain, — some say 30 miles, — there is a beautiful beach here of a great extent, the outlet forms a considerable stream of a gentle descent. Dist. to-day 30 miles.

September 22d. — Marched at sunrise. The land & timber the same as yesterday. Arrived at the outlet of a lake, that appeared nearly of the same dimensions of the Wasco, halted a few minutes & then descended into a very deep valley, where there was a considerable brook, then ascended a very high hill, & the land & woods nearly the same as before. Arrived at Onandaga about sunset; this was the capital of the Onandaga nation & was destroyed last Spring by a detachment of our army from Fort Schuyler, under the command of Coll. Vanschaick — Dist. 30 miles.

September 23d. — Marched a little after sunrise, crossed the Onandaga River & ascended the hill ; The woods continued open for five miles. Our advance parties discovered two Indians on the path before them, who immediately fled & left one of their packs. The woods then was thick, & the land very good in most places & filled with a number of crystal rivulets, halted at Sunken Spring in the road. Arrived at Canaseraga, a handsome village & Capital of the Tuscarora Tribe — The Inhabitants appear very hospitable & presented us with boiled corn & eels, with every other thing their town afforded, they likewise congratulated us on the success of our arms & insisted on our tarrying with them all night. After staying with them sometime, we marched about six miles further & encamped in an old field. Dist. 31 miles.

September 24-th. — Marched at sunrise, the land very good. Arrived at the Oneida Castle, about 9 o'clock, the inhabitants received us very kindly, made a genteel apology for their not being apprised of our coming and also congratulated us on our success. Halted a short time & then marched for Fort Schuyler, where we arrived at 3 o'clock, met with a genteel reception from the garrisons — dist. 26 miles. This is a regular work with four Bastions, in which are several pieces of cannon, is beautifully situated about 400 yards from the Mohawk River on the west side, the wall is high, the ditch wide & well picketed, a strong gate & draw-bridge with one sally port, it was built by Stanwix, last war, but is now greatly improved & has changed its name to Fort Schuyler, famous for the noble defence that was made in it by Col. Gansewoort in 1777. At present it is garrisoned by the First 1ST. York Regt. under the command of Col. Van Dyke.

September 25th. — Marched at 4 o'clock P.M., having detached an officer with some men in two batteaux, which contained our baggage and provisions, with orders to meet us in the evening at our encampment. The roads muddy, passed the place where Gen. Herkimer's battle happened; the skulls & bones of many of the unfortunate victims are still to be found. Encamped at Arisca — the extreme dry season prevented our boats from arriving. Rain in the evening — dist. 8 miles.

September 26th. — Marched before sunrise. Crossed the River at old Fort Schuyler, dist. 8 miles, then we arrived near Germantown — here was the first inhabitants we had seen for three months — the people very inhospitable — arrived at Fort Dayton on the beautiful German Flats — then proceeded over the River to Fort Hackeman (about a mile), where we were well received by Colonel Van Rensselear, Comd. of the Garrisons, where we tarried all night.

September 27th. — Marched at 9 o'clock, (having previously detached some men in batteaux to carry off the remainder of the Mohawk tribe that lived on Schohare Creek), sent our baggage in batteaux. Crossed the River at Col. Clock's, a little rain, lodged at Col. "Wormwood's.

September 28th. — Rain in the morning. Marched at 8 o'clock. Arrived at the old Fort at Johnston Hall at sunset, dist. 26 miles.

September 29th. — Marched at 8 o'clock — Arrived at Schanectady at 1 o'clock — Arrived in Albany at dark, very dirty and tired, dist. 39 miles.

Remained in Albany until the 7th of October, when we shipped our Baggage on board a sloop bound for New Windsor, then set out in company with Capt. Machin — Rode to Conines, where we lodged, dist. 20 miles.

October 8th. — Continued our journey, arrived in Esopus at sunset, from there we went to " Green Hill" where we lodged — dist. 44 miles.

October 9th. — Lay by to day — Treated very politely by the family.

October 10th. — Set out this morning towards New "Windsor, parted with Capt. Machin, arrived at Little Britain.

October 11th. — Set out for New Windsor, where I met some gentlemen of our party, with whom I went for orders to Head Quarters at West Point. Returned in the evening, hard rain.

October 12th. — Encamped with the detachment of artillery that was encamped there, who treated me very politely.

October 15th. — Saw several Gentlemen from Gen. Sullivan's Army.

October 16th & 17th. — Nothing material happened.

October 18th. — "Went to the Park at Chester, staid there two days & then returned.

October 27th. — Nothing worthy of notice happened until the 27th, when I went to "West Point, where I saw a number of old acquaintances, staid there two days & then returned.

October 30th. — Received a number of letters from several gentlemen arrived from different parts — Ordered to hold ourselves in readiness to join our corps.

October 31st. — Waited for further orders.

November 7th. — Set out for New Windsor with our baggage, in company with Capt. Machin & St. Cebra (the detachment from the York line having marched the day before to join the western army in the Clove), lodged in the Clove. Met Capt. Porter who informed us the army had marched for Pompton.

November 8th. — Marched at 9 o'clock, lodged near Ringwood, dist. 22 miles.

November 9th. — Marched at 10, arrived at Pompton about 1 o'clock P.M., where we found the army.

November 10th. — Lay by; in the afternoon we shifted our ground & encamped in the woods, very cold in the evening.

November 12th. — The army put on half allowance of flour.

November 15th. — Capt. McClure arrived from Head Quarters.

Received at Pompton of Lieut. Robt. Parker, our pay for the months of May, June, July & August last :

Michal Royall, Sergt	40 dollars
Archd. McFair, Sergt.	40 dollars
John Kelly, Bomb'r,	36 dollars
John Johnston,	36 dollars
John McGregor, Sergt.	40 dollars
Arthur Gillas,	33 1/3 dollars
George Stewart,	33 1/3 dollars
Saml. Laughlan,	33 1/3 dollars
Iac. Bennington,	33 1/3 dollars
Jas. Ryburn,	33 1/3 dollars
John Mark,	33 1/3 dollars
Robert Jeff,	33 1/3 dollars
Alex. Martin,	33 1/3 dollars
Reuben Benjon,	33 1/3 dollars
Benj. Phipps,	33 1/3 dollars
Jas. Wilson,	33 1/3 dollars
John Dunn,	33 1/3 dollars

Received at Pompton of Lieut Parker, the sums annexed to our names as part of our pay & subsistence for the months of May June July & August last :

Andrew Porter, Capt. Art'y,	348 2/3 dollars
Jas. McClure, Capt. Lieut. Art'y,	207 2/3 dollars
Ezra Patterson,	207 2/3 dollars
Ezekiel Howell,	207 2/3 dollars
Robt. Parker, Lieut.	207 2/3 dollars

November 17th. — Capt. Porter returned from Head Quarters.

November 19th. — Capt. Porter set out for Philadelphia; ordered to hold ourselves in readiness to march.

November 22d. — "No flour to be had for the Troops.

November 24-th. — Marched at 2 o'clock. Encamped on Pompton plains, near the Church, dist. 6 miles.

November 25th. — Marched at 8 o'clock. The roads very bad & the weather cold, encamped near Hanover, dist. 14 miles.

November 26th. — I went to Morris Town ; about 11 o'clock it began to snow & continued all day, at night it cleared up very cold.

November 30th. — The First Maryland Brigade arrived to- day.

December 1st. — His Excellency arrived at Morristown to-day; very severe storm of hail & snow all day.

December 3d. — This morning we marched through Morristown & encamped near Kembles. Great part of the Army arrived to day.

December 4-th. — Marched back within two miles of Morristown & encamped there; the army continued to move to their ground.

December 5th. — Snow all day and the weather very cold.

December 6th. — Marched this morning to Morristown & joined the Grand Park, which lay about a mile west of that place — encamped there, the snow knee deep & the weather very cold.

Head Quarters— New Windsor

Jan'y 1st 1781

The non Commissioned Officers & Matrosses of the Independent Companies of Artillery, lately commanded by Capt. Coran, are to be added to, & incorporated with the company lately commanded by Capt. Porter now in the 2d Reg't of Artillery — And the non Commissioned Officers & Matrosses of the Company Commanded by Capt. Freeman, are to be added to & incorporated with Capt. Simonds' Company in said Reg't. Capt Porter's and Capt Simonds' Companies are to be levelled with the men of the two companies which are incorporated with them & being raised by Pennsylvania, are to be added to Coll. Proctor's Reg't of Artillery.

The Officers of the two Companies com'd. by Capt. Porter & Capt. Simonds, are to be arraingned in Col. Proctor's Regt. agreeable to the rank they now hold.

Journal of Lieutenant Robert Parker

Cornwallis' Soliloquy. 1

Indulgent Fortune, by whose hand,
I've led my chosen British band
To conquest, through all war's alarms,
And victory, hovering round my arms;
Of my success, Great Britain rung,
And echoed with the feats I'd done,
Ambitious, whou'd excel in praise
They offer up their tuneful lays.

Successive I had roll'd along
While British bards repeat the song
But wild ambition fired my breast,
And dreams of honor broke my rest;
With pompous speech & great parade,
Some converts to my arms I made
But dire distress I kept for those
Who dare my vig'rous arms oppose.

But now, alas! all joys are fled,
And laurel wreaths that crowned my head,
Their native hue have quickly lost,
While I'm on Fortune's billows tossed;
York's narrow sphere points to my bounds
Contracted lines describe my rounds,
United arms my works oppose

While raging fire my bosom glows.

Mark! how in circling eddies rise,
The smoke sulphurious to the skies,
Hark! how the cannon shakes the pole
And speaks loud terror to my soul;

See yonder shot spread carnage round,
And angry shells tear up the ground,
Bellona's thunder sounds afar,
Ye Gods! are these the scenes of war?

Such toils as these I can't endure,
My cause no longer is secure,
I'll straight resign my tarnished arms,
Nor wait another night's alarms;
Safe from the terrors of a storm,
Or fierce assault of rising morn,
Quickly embark for Albion's shore
Nor ever dream of conquest more.

---

1 Composed by Lieutenant Robert Parker, who witnessed the surrender of Cornwallis's army to the American army*

Other New York military books from New York History Review

A Soldier's Story: Prison Life and Other Incidents in the War of 1861-1865 - Elmira Prison Camp
by Miles O. Sherrill

To War and Back - Carl Albert Janowski's Army Diary 1918-1919

In Their Honor - Soldiers of the Confederacy - The Elmira Prison Camp
by Diane Janowski

Diary of A Tar Heel Confederate Soldier
by L. Leon

The Elmira Prison Camp, a History of the Military Prison at Elmira, New York July 6, 1864 - July 10, 1865 with New Appendix
by Clay Holmes

www.ingramcontent.com/pod-product-compliance
Lightning Source LLC
Chambersburg PA
CBHW030005050426
42451CB00006B/124